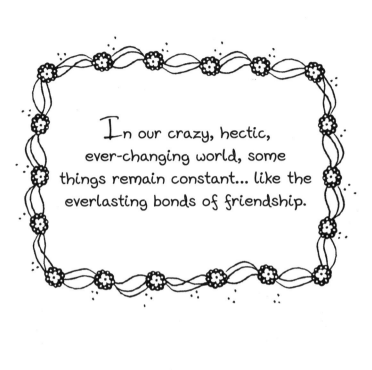

In our crazy, hectic,
ever-changing world, some
things remain constant... like the
everlasting bonds of friendship.

ISBN: 978-1-68088-410-4

Children of the Inner Light is a registered trademark. Used under license.

▌▌and Blue Mountain Press are registered in U.S. Patent and Trademark Office. Certain trademarks are used under license.

Printed in China.
First Printing: 2022

✿ This book is printed on recycled paper.

This book is printed on paper that has been specially produced to be acid free (neutral pH) and contains no groundwood or unbleached pulp. It conforms with the requirements of the American National Standards Institute, Inc., so as to ensure that this book will last and be enjoyed by future generations.

Blue Mountain Arts, Inc.
P.O. Box 4549, Boulder, Colorado 80306

Girlfriends
Always & Forever
There for Each Other

In Each Other
We Find Strength

Marci

Blue Mountain Press™
Boulder, Colorado

Girlfriends
Always & Forever
There for Each Other

I never take for granted what we have — a lasting friendship built on all the things that make life so special. We've shared both the good and the bad — we've listened intently to each other's troubles... and we've shared in the triumphs and successes of life that make it so joyous. When I stop and think of the really important things in life — all those things that bring real and lasting happiness — I'm thankful to have the friend I have in you.

We're More
Than Friends...
We're Sisters in Spirit.®

You are everything I could ever want in a friend. When I want to talk... you listen. When I am down... you encourage me. When I am happy... you share my joy. When I am sad... your hug tells me everything will be okay. You know my deepest hopes and share my greatest dreams.

You are a bright light... an arm around my shoulder... a word of encouragement when I need one... and my friend.

Friendship Is One of Life's Greatest Treasures

Through the gift of friendship, we are given the opportunity to give and receive love while traveling the journey of life. We share our hopes and dreams and learn about our best selves as we meet the challenge to give support and to be there when we are needed.

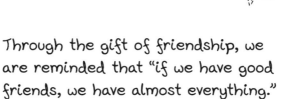

Through the gift of friendship, we are reminded that "if we have good friends, we have almost everything." I am so glad that I have you!

FAITH
HOPE
LOVE

I'm So Thankful for the Day Our Paths Crossed

Our journeys sometimes bring us to a place where we meet someone special. This person brings a wisdom to our conversations as they tell us the things we need to hear. They bring hope to difficult times by shining the light of a positive perspective — and they become, through the sharing of themselves, one of our most cherished friends. I will always hold the gift of your friendship close to my heart and be thankful for the day we met.

Our Friendship Was Meant to Be

Friendship happens when two special people meet and connect heart and soul. There develops an understanding of what is in each other's heart that transcends words. There is a nurturing of the spirit that is mutual, an exchange of love and support that is essential, and a sense of belonging and knowing that their friendship was meant to be. I know we will be friends for life!

You Are a Beautiful Part of My Story

Friendship gives us a path to be our best selves through the telling of our stories. Through the joys and heartbreaks we share, we learn that we are not alone. Through the love and support we give, we tap into the lessons that we have learned. You are such a special part of my story — and have given me so much as my friend.

I'll Stand
By You...
Rain or Shine

There are times in our lives when our inner struggles are so great that we can't really express how we feel. These are the times when we need to know that someone is there for us, that someone cares about what is best for us, and that someone loves us no matter what. Remember, I am always here for you... I will always love you... and I'll stand by you, no matter how hard life gets, until the light is shining again.

In Each Other We Find Strength

We share a special bond as women —
we know what it means to give so much
of ourselves to others. I can share with
you my hopes and dreams and know
that you will understand.

We've cried, we've laughed, we've failed, we've soared. We've seen the highs and lows of life together and given each other the strength to endure... survive... triumph... and know the power of being a woman.

When I Think
About Friendship,
I Think About You

When I think about friendship and how important it is to our sense of happiness and well-being, I realize that over a lifetime we really only find a special few. Then I think about you and what a good friend you are and always have been to me. Through thick and thin, you are there by my side... When I lose sight of the big picture, you point me in the right direction... When life gets too crazy, you know how to make me laugh. I'm so grateful to have a friend like you.

You're My Angel
Without Wings

Sometimes the stars line up in such a way to ensure that we meet people who are meant to be in our lives. I feel certain this is what happened the day I met you. God sent you with a message of hope. Maybe you didn't even realize that you carried that message each time you reminded me God has a plan or sent me a prayer... but I've always felt the blessing of having you in my life. You are my angel without wings.

We've Shared
So Much as Women
and as Friends

There are some moments that we just can't put into words, and when we try, we end up with laughter... or tears... or both together rolled into one indescribable emotion called joy. These times become our most treasured memories because they've been shared with someone very important and loved in our lives. Thank you for giving me so many of these special moments — I'll never forget all the times we shared... the memories we made... or the fun we had along the way.

♥ ♥ ♥

We Are Family
in All the Ways
That Matter

Friends

When it comes to thoughts of family, you are always in my heart. You are there whenever I need you — sometimes to share the joys of life, sometimes to help me get through a difficult time. I can count on you to just listen when my thoughts overwhelm me, and you never forget to remind me that everything will be okay. The ways you show me you care are all the ways of family, and I want you to know that I think of you as a part of mine.

We Will Be There
for Each Other
No Matter What

Even though we are different in a lot of ways, we are alike in ways that are so important. Our values, our beliefs, and the things we hold dear like family, love, and faith create the gift of an everlasting bond. We always know we can turn to each other in times of need — and that we will each be there to support the other through life's trials. The good times give us a chance to share all the little blessings of life and make me so glad that we have each other.

We Share an Everlasting Bond

We made a special connection long ago, at a time when dreams were being born in our hearts. We shared all those things that help forge an everlasting bond — hopes, values, good times, and struggles. We learned so much about life through the talks, the laughs, and sometimes the tears. I will always cherish our friendship and give thanks for the day you became my friend!

Your Friendship
Is a Blessing
in My Life

For all the times you've lifted me up,
given me hope, saved me from myself,
loved me anyway, laughed with me,

cried with me,
railed at the
world with me,
shared my joys
and my sorrows,
and been
my friend...

For all the times when I've reached out and you've always found time for me — to listen, commiserate, or say "It's all good"...

For all the times when I've doubted myself, the world, and my purpose in it — but you've said, "I think you're amazing!"...

There's no better friend than that — there's no better friend than you.

Thank You for Being My Friend

It's easy to be a friend when the sun shines, but you've been there for the storms, too — holding my hand, offering hope, and always reminding me that everything will work out in the end. There is so much between us and so much we've experienced together — triumphs, losses, and the dreams we held for our lives. I'll never forget the unconditional love expressed through our friendship. I wish you all the good things that life will bring... because you are so wonderful and true.

You Are Always in My Thoughts and Prayers

Whenever life gets you down or sends challenges you think are too big to handle, remember this: I am thinking of you and wishing you the best... I am praying for you and hoping you remember that you are in God's care... and I am wrapping my arms around you with my heart, sending hugs and prayers your way!

Our Friendship Means Everything to Me

Love

Friendship means having someone to give you a hug when you need one.

Friendship means having someone to love you through good times and bad.

Friendship means having someone to share life's joys and to dry the tears through life's sorrows.

Friendship means that someone is there to shine a light on the path ahead... and shed some light on the path behind.

Friendship means that there are people who will always love you no matter what.

I'm so grateful for the gift of our friendship and for the blessing in my life that is you.

About Marci

Marci began her career by
hand painting floral designs
on clothing. No one was more
surprised than she was when
one day, in a single burst of
inspiration and a completely
new and different art style,
her delightful characters sprang from her pen! "Their
wild and crazy hair is a sign of strength," she thought,
"and their crooked little smiles are endearing." She
quickly identified the charming characters as Mother,
Daughter, Sister, Father, Son, Friend, and so on until
all the people and places in life were filled. Then,
with her own loved ones in mind, she wrote a true
and special sentiment to each one. This would be the
beginning of a wonderful success story, which today
still finds Marci writing each and every one of her
verses in this same personal way.

Marci is a self-taught artist who has always enjoyed
writing and art. She is thrilled to see how her
delightful characters and universal messages of
love have touched the hearts and lives of people
everywhere. Her distinctive designs can also be found
on Blue Mountain Arts greeting cards, calendars,
bookmarks, and other gift items.

To learn more about Marci, look for Children of the
Inner Light on Facebook or visit her website:
www.MARCIonline.com.